AI and Your Health

How Technology is Changing Medicine

M.A. Gorre

Contents

Introduction

In the annals of human history, some milestones have dramatically shifted the course of civilizations—the fire was harnessed, electricity was tamed, and now, we stand on the precipice of another transformational moment: the era of Artificial Intelligence. Just as fire and electricity fundamentally changed all aspects of human life, from how we cook our food to how we illuminate our nights, AI promises to instigate a paradigm shift that will ripple through every fibre of our society, including the very way we understand, treat, and conceptualize healthcare.

As a nurse deeply embedded in the current healthcare system, I can attest to the profound ways AI will revolutionize medicine. It's not merely a matter of technology making tasks more accessible or more efficient—though it undoubtedly will—it's a leap forward that will enhance the precision, accuracy, and effectiveness of medical diagnosis and treatment. This book aims to dissect that transformation, breaking down complex algorithms and medical jargon into a language accessible to everyone, from healthcare professionals to the general public.

AI has the potential to democratize healthcare in unprecedented ways. It promises cost-effectiveness, making high-quality healthcare more accessible to people across social and economic strata. It offers speed, enabling quicker diagnosis and treatment, which can be lifesaving in critical cases. And it ensures accuracy, minimizing human error in everything from prescription dosages to surgical procedures.

As with any significant shift, it's natural for skepticism and apprehension to permeate public perception. However, this book seeks to illuminate not only the profound benefits but also the ethical considerations and responsibilities that come with wielding such transformative power. We'll delve into real-world applications, scrutinize existing challenges, and explore emerging trends. We'll examine what the AI-driven future of healthcare could look like and discuss how to prepare for this inevitable change.

This book is not just a guide but a dialogue, an invitation to be part of one of the most crucial conversations of our time. So, as you turn these pages, I invite you to ponder, critique, and engage with the material, for the AI era is not a distant future but an evolving present. And the sooner we understand its potential and limitations, the better equipped we'll be to harness its extraordinary capabilities for the greater good.

Welcome to "AI and Your Health: How Technology is Changing Medicine." Let's embark on this journey together.

Chapter One

Current State of Healthcare

As we stand on the brink of a new era where Artificial Intelligence (AI) promises to revolutionize healthcare, it's crucial to take stock of the current state of healthcare systems globally. Below are some essential facets that encapsulate the existing landscape, challenges, and opportunities in healthcare:

Accessibility and Inequality:

1. **Rural-Urban Divide**: Access to quality healthcare is not uniformly distributed. While urban areas generally have better healthcare services, rural regions often lack facilities and specialists.

2. **Global Inequalities**: Healthcare accessibility and quality can vary dramatically between developed and developing countries, leading to disparate health outcomes.

Cost and Efficiency:

1. **Rising Costs**: Healthcare costs are ballooning worldwide due to multiple factors, including an aging population, the high price of medical equipment, and expensive treatments and medications.

2. **Operational Inefficiencies**: Redundant paperwork, administrative overhead, and fragmented communication systems often lead to inefficiencies that compromise patient care.

Technological Advancements:

1. **Telemedicine**: Virtual consultations have gained significant traction, especially during the COVID-19 pandemic, as an alternative to in-person visits.

2. **Electronic Health Records (EHRs)**: While EHRs have streamlined data management to some extent, their full potential remains untapped due to interoperability issues and privacy concerns.

Patient Experience:

1. **Patient-Centric Care**: There is an increasing emphasis on patient-centric care, though the execution still varies from one healthcare system to another.

2. **Mental Health**: While there is a growing acknowledgment of mental health as an integral part of overall health, it is often stigmatized and under-resourced compared to physical health.

Quality and Outcomes:

1. **Standardization of Care**: Efforts like evidence-based medicine aim to standardize treatments and improve care quality. However, much more work needs to be done in this area.

2. **Outcome Metrics**: The shift towards outcome-based healthcare over fee-for-service models is slowly gaining momentum.

Regulatory Environment:

1. **Data Privacy**: Regulations like GDPR in Europe and HIPAA in the United States aim to protect patient data, but they also present data sharing and interoperability challenges.

2. **Ethical Concerns**: Medical malpractice, informed consent, and equitable access to medical advances continue to pose ethical challenges.

Future Outlook:

1. **Aging Population**: As life expectancy increases, healthcare

systems must adapt to cater to an older population likely to have more complex health needs.

2. **Pandemic Preparedness**: The COVID-19 pandemic has exposed vulnerabilities in healthcare systems globally, emphasizing the need for better pandemic preparedness and response mechanisms.

The current state of healthcare presents a mix of challenges and opportunities. While there are undeniable problems relating to accessibility, costs, and quality, there are also unprecedented possibilities enabled by technological advancements. As AI and other innovative technologies become more integrated into healthcare, there is an enormous potential to address many of these challenges and redefine what healthcare can achieve.

By closely examining the current state of healthcare, we can better appreciate the transformative power that AI could bring into this vital sector.

Chapter Two

Challenges and Opportunities

Navigating the Complex Landscape of AI in Healthcare

T he fusion of AI and healthcare presents an intricate tableau of challenges and opportunities. As we stand at the threshold of what could be a significant paradigm shift in medicine, it's crucial to delve into these aspects to understand the full scope and implications of this revolution.

Challenges:

1. **Data Privacy and Security:**

    - **Issue**: With AI algorithms requiring vast amounts of data, ensuring the privacy and security of patient information becomes paramount.

- **Potential Solutions**: Implementation of robust encryption methods, stringent data access controls, and regular audits.

2. Algorithmic Bias:

- **Issue**: If not adequately trained, AI algorithms can perpetuate or exacerbate healthcare disparities.

- **Potential Solutions**: More inclusive data collection and continuous monitoring for bias.

3. Interoperability:

- **Issue**: The sharing of data between different healthcare systems remains a significant challenge, affecting the performance of AI algorithms.

- **Potential Solutions**: Development of universal standards and protocols for data exchange.

4. Regulatory Hurdles:

- **Issue**: Navigating the complicated landscape of healthcare regulations can be challenging for AI adoption.

- **Potential Solutions**: Collaboration between tech firms, healthcare providers, and regulatory bodies to create AI-friendly policy frameworks.

5. Cost of Implementation:

- **Issue**: The initial cost of implementing AI solutions can be high, especially for smaller healthcare providers.

○ **Potential Solutions**: Cost-benefit analyses to show long-term savings and benefits and scalable AI solutions tailored to various budget sizes.

6. Ethical Concerns:

○ **Issue**: Questions about who is responsible when an AI makes a mistake or ethical considerations about AI's role in decision-making can arise.

○ **Potential Solutions**: Clear guidelines for accountability and a robust ethical framework for AI's role in healthcare.

Opportunities:

1. Improved Diagnostics:

○ **Potential**: AI can significantly speed up and increase the accuracy of diagnostics, from image recognition in radiology to predictive analytics for disease outbreaks.

2. Enhanced Personalization:

○ **Potential**: Tailoring treatment plans to individuals based on comprehensive data analysis can result in more effective and efficient healthcare.

3. Operational Efficiency:

○ **Potential**: Automating routine tasks can free healthcare providers to focus more on patient care, ultimately improving outcomes and satisfaction.

4. Remote Monitoring and Telehealth:

- ○ **Potential**: AI-powered monitoring tools can offer better home care solutions and enhance telehealth services, bridging gaps in healthcare accessibility.

5. Drug Discovery and Development:

- ○ **Potential**: AI algorithms can analyze complex biochemical interactions, substantially speeding up drug discovery and time-to-market.

6. Global Health Initiatives:

- ○ **Potential**: AI can help optimize resource allocation in global health initiatives, making it possible to do more with less.

Integrating AI into healthcare will be a complex but potentially transformative journey. Both challenges and opportunities abound, and navigating this duality will require concerted efforts from healthcare providers, technologists, policymakers, and patients alike. By addressing the challenges head-on while leveraging the opportunities, we can usher in a new era of healthcare that is more efficient, equitable, and patient-centric than ever before.

Chapter Three

What is AI?

The terms Artificial Intelligence (AI), Machine Learning (ML), and Deep Learning (DL) are often used interchangeably, but they are not synonymous. Understanding these terms and their nuanced differences is essential for grasping how they contribute to healthcare. Below is an outline that defines these terms and explains their application in the healthcare sector.

Artificial Intelligence (AI):

Definition:

- AI is a broad field of computer science focused on creating systems that can perform tasks that typically require human intelligence. These tasks include problem-solving, speech recognition, decision-making, and more.

Application in Healthcare:

- AI in healthcare can range from automated customer service bots answering patient queries to complex algorithms analyzing radiology images.

- AI helps in predictive analytics, offering forecasts on patient admissions, which can help in better resource management.

- AI-driven robotic surgery is becoming more precise, allowing for minimally invasive procedures.

Machine Learning (ML):

Definition:

- Machine Learning is a subfield of AI that allows the system to learn from data rather than being explicitly programmed. In other words, ML algorithms use statistical methods to enable machines to improve with experience.

Application in Healthcare:

- ML models can analyze large datasets to identify patterns or anomalies, such as detecting potential tumours in X-ray images.

- ML can be used in predictive modelling to identify patients at high risk for certain conditions like diabetes or heart disease.

- Drug discovery and genetic research are greatly expedited with ML algorithms that analyze complex biochemical interactions.

Deep Learning (DL):

Definition:

- Deep Learning is a subset of ML and involves neural networks with three or more layers. These neural networks attempt to simulate the behaviour of the human brain to "learn" from large amounts of data.

Application in Healthcare:

- Deep Learning is particularly effective in processing unstructured data, like that found in EHR (Electronic Health Records).

- It's commonly used in image recognition tasks such as identifying abnormalities in MRI, CT scans, and X-rays with high accuracy.

- Deep Learning models are used for real-time language translation in international healthcare settings, breaking down linguistic barriers in patient care.

Differences:

- **AI** is the broadest term, encompassing any simulation of human intelligence by machines.

- **ML** is a method to achieve AI specifically focused on developing algorithms that can learn from data.

- **DL** is a specialized form of ML that uses neural networks with three or more layers to analyze various data factors.

Understanding these terms and their differences helps us appreciate the depth and breadth of possibilities that AI, ML, and DL bring to healthcare. From improving patient outcomes and healthcare delivery to automating mundane tasks, these technologies have begun transforming how we understand and approach health and well-being.

Chapter Four

Ethical Considerations in AI and Medicine

As AI continues to make inroads into healthcare, ethical considerations have risen to the forefront of discussions among policymakers, medical professionals, and technologists. While the technology has the potential to revolutionize healthcare delivery and outcomes, it also presents challenges that need to be carefully navigated. Here are some of the critical ethical dimensions:

Patient Privacy:

1. **Data Consent**: Before AI can analyze patient data, proper consent must be obtained. However, the complex nature of AI algorithms often makes it difficult for patients to fully understand the implications of giving their consent.

2. **Data Security**: AI systems require vast amounts of data to function effectively. This data, often susceptible, must be stored and transmitted securely to prevent unauthorized access and potential misuse.

3. **Ownership and Control**: Who owns the data once AI algorithms process it? What control do patients have over their data once it's part of a larger dataset?

4. **Third-Party Sharing**: There are concerns over whether healthcare data could be shared with third parties like insurance companies or advertisers, potentially affecting patient privacy adversely.

AI Bias and Fairness:

1. **Data Bias**: If the data used to train AI algorithms is biased, the AI system will perpetuate that bias. For example, a system introduced primarily on data from one racial or ethnic group may not perform as well for others.

2. **Decision-making Bias**: Bias can also be built into the decision-making processes of AI systems. For instance, if an algorithm is designed to prioritize cost-saving, it might neglect to recommend more expensive but potentially life-saving treatments.

3. **Algorithmic Transparency**: It's crucial to make AI algorithms as transparent as possible to identify and rectify any biasesintense. However, many current algorithms, especially deep learning models, are often described as "black boxes"

that are difficult to interpret.

4. **Fair Access**: As AI systems often require significant resources to implement and maintain, there is a risk of widening the healthcare gap between well-funded institutions and
those lacking in resources, affecting equitable access to quality healthcare.

Accountability:

1. **Error Responsibility**: Who is responsible if an AI system
makes an error that affects patient care? Is it the developers,
the medical practitioners, or the institution?

2. **Ethical Training**: Developers and users of medical AI
should be trained in ethical considerations to guide the development and deployment of these systems.

3. **Regulatory Oversight**: To ensure ethical compliance, AI
systems in healthcare may need to be regulated at multiple levels, including governmental bodies and medical ethics
committees.

4. **Public Trust**: Earning and maintaining the public's trust is
crucial for the widespread acceptance and successful implementation of AI in healthcare.

Understanding and addressing these ethical considerations are not
just supplementary aspects of AI in healthcare; they are fundamental
to the responsible development and deployment of AI technologies
in medical settings. Failure to navigate these ethical waters carefully

could undermine the vast potential benefits that AI could bring to healthcare globally.

Chapter Five

AI Historical Perspective

AI in Medicine:

T he journey of AI in medicine is an intriguing tale of innovation, setbacks, and resurgence. From humble beginnings to its current burgeoning state, AI's role in medicine has been in a constant state of evolution. Below, we examine some landmark moments and early uses that have shaped this relationship.

Early Pioneers:

1. **ELIZA (1966)**: One of the earliest examples, ELIZA, was a computer program created by Joseph Weizenbaum that emulated a Rogerian psychotherapist. Although simplistic by today's standards, it was a pioneering experiment in natural language processing and the human-machine interface.

2. **Dendral (1965)**: Initially a project in mass spectrometry and isotope labelling, Dendral was one of the first expert systems and laid the groundwork for developing subsequent medical expert systems.

Expert Systems in the 1970s and 1980s:

1. **MYCIN (1972)**: Developed at Stanford University, MYCIN was designed to diagnose bacterial infections and recommend antibiotic treatments. Despite its limitations, it outperformed human experts in some cases and sparked interest in the capabilities of AI in medical diagnostics.

2. **Internist-I (1970s)**: This system was created to assist general internists in diagnosing complex cases. It was one of the first AI systems that aimed to mimic the decision-making process of human doctors.

3. **CADUCEUS (1980s)**: An evolution of an earlier DxC system, CADUCEUS aimed to diagnose medical conditions. Although it did not achieve widespread adoption, it set the stage for future diagnostic AI systems.

Image Recognition and Radiology:

1. **1980s-1990s**: Early attempts to apply AI in radiology existed but were largely unsuccessful due to limited computational power and lack of sufficient data.

2. **2000s**: With advancements in machine learning and hard-

ware, AI began to show promise in image recognition tasks, notably in mammography and other types of medical imaging.

The Rise of Machine Learning and Big Data:

1. **Early 2000s**: As machine learning algorithms became more sophisticated, AI began to find applications in various specialized medical fields, such as genetics, oncology, and neurology.

2. **Late 2000s and 2010s**: The era of Big Data offered unprecedented opportunities for AI in medicine. Complex algorithms could now be trained on large datasets, leading to more accurate and personalized medicine.

Notable Milestones:

1. **IBM Watson for Oncology (2010s)**: Watson was one of the first AI systems that sought to assist oncologists in diagnosing and treating cancer, although its efficacy has been a subject of debate.

2. **FDA Approvals (2010s-2020s)**: Various AI-powered medical devices and software have received FDA approval, marking a regulatory milestone for the field.

Contemporary Scene:

1. **COVID-19 Pandemic**: AI has managed the COVID-19 crisis, from diagnostics to drug discovery.

2. **Ethical Concerns and Policy**: As AI becomes more integrated into healthcare, ethical considerations like data privacy and algorithmic bias are gaining attention.

Looking back, the journey of AI in medicine has been fraught with challenges but also ripe with opportunities. With the last decade's exponential rise in capabilities and applications, it has oscillated between skepticism and optimism. The story of AI in medicine is still being written, but its historical perspective offers invaluable lessons as we navigate this promising yet complex landscape.

Chapter Six

The Maturation of AI in Medicine

Evolution Over Time

T he evolution of AI in medicine can be likened to the trajectory of a technology coming of age. From a novel concept rife with possibilities and limitations to a mature, integral part of modern healthcare, AI's journey has been marked by significant milestones, adaptations, and leaps in capabilities. Below is an overview of how AI has evolved in the realm of medicine:

Infancy Stage: The Birth of Concept (1960s-1980s)

- **Initial Enthusiasm**: The nascent years saw the development of rudimentary expert systems like ELIZA and MYCIN, sparking optimism about AI's role in healthcare.

- **Technology Gap**: Despite the potential, the technological infrastructure was not ready to support the lofty ambitions.

- **Focus on Narrow Applications**: The technology was mainly deployed in isolated cases or to manage specific tasks, like bacterial identification and primary mental health assessments.

Childhood Stage: Learning and Growth (1990s)

- **Emerging Technologies**: The 1990s brought advances in machine learning techniques, data storage, and computational power.

- **Early Adaptation in Imaging**: AI technologies started emerging in medical imaging, although widespread adoption was still a far-off goal.

- **The Internet Boom**: The rise of the Internet provided a new platform for health informatics, although it didn't immediately translate to AI adoption in medicine.

Adolescent Stage: Pushing Boundaries (2000s)

- **Data Explosion**: The 2000s saw a surge in electronic health records, genomic data, and other forms of Big Data.

- **Specialized Applications**: AI started to penetrate specialized medicine, particularly in fields like oncology and neurology, though not without skepticism.

- **Initial Regulatory Steps**: Some AI solutions began receiving approvals from governing bodies like the FDA, although the pathway remained nebulous.

Adulthood Stage: Real-world Integration (2010s-2020s)

- **AI and Analytics**: AI technologies have become increasingly sophisticated and can handle complex analytics, including predictive modelling.

- **Standardization and Regulation**: Regulatory bodies began to formulate guidelines for AI in medicine, making it easier for innovations to reach the clinical setting.

- **Commercialization**: Tech giants and startups started investing heavily in healthcare AI, leading to commercial product surges.

- **Ethical Considerations**: As AI's impact grew, so did the ethical questions surrounding its use, including concerns about data privacy and algorithmic bias.

The Future: A New Horizon

- **AI-First Healthcare**: A shift towards an AI-centric healthcare system that leverages data to improve patient outcomes and system efficiencies.

- **Global Health**: AI has the potential to revolutionize healthcare on a global scale, providing resource-optimized solutions in low-income settings.

- **Human-AI Collaboration**: Rather than replacing health-care providers, AI is expected to act as a supplement, augmenting human capabilities.

The story of AI in medicine is a narrative of constant evolution, adaptation, and maturation. Each stage of its life has brought challenges and breakthroughs, setting the stage for a future full of promise, complexities, and transformative potential.

Chapter Seven

The Fusion of Two Worlds: AI and Healthcare

A t first glance, Artificial Intelligence and healthcare might appear as disparate fields—one rooted in cold computation and the other in the warm touch of a caregiver. However, as we delve deeper, it becomes evident that these two worlds are not just intersecting; they are fusing in ways that profoundly change both fields. This fusion brings many opportunities and challenges that promise to redefine healthcare as we know it.

Opportunities:

1. **Efficiency:** Healthcare systems across the globe are under immense pressure to cater to an ever-growing population. AI can streamline administrative tasks and accelerate diagnoses, allowing medical professionals to focus more on patient care.

2. **Accuracy:** Machine learning algorithms can sift through massive datasets far more quickly and accurately than the human eye, reducing errors in everything from prescriptions to surgical procedures.

3. **Personalization:** AI enables hyper-personalized healthcare by sifting through a patient's medical history, genetic make-up, and lifestyle choices to recommend the most effective treatments.

4. **Resource Allocation:** AI can predict patient inflow in emergency wards, the possible spread of diseases, and even the life cycle of a pandemic, allowing for more intelligent resource allocation.

5. **Global Reach:** Telemedicine equipped with AI diagnostic tools can bring quality healthcare to remote or underprivileged regions, levelling the playing field like never before.

Challenges:

1. **Data Security:** With significant data comes great responsibility. The medical data that AI systems need to operate are sensitive and must be protected to ensure patient confidentiality.

2. **Ethical Concerns:** The introduction of AI in healthcare raises ethical questions around bias, fairness, and the 'human' touch in caregiving.

3. **Regulatory Hurdles:** Regulatory frameworks need to

adapt for AI to be fully realized in healthcare. This involves exhaustive clinical trials and creating standards for AI healthcare applications.

4. **Adoption and Trust:** There's a learning curve involved for healthcare providers and patients alike to trust AI systems, and not all are willing to navigate it.

5. **Job Displacement:** While AI can handle repetitive tasks, there's concern over the displacement of healthcare jobs. The challenge is to integrate AI in a way that augments rather than replaces human skills.

The Way Forward:

The fusion of AI and healthcare is inevitable and, arguably, necessary. We'll explore these opportunities and challenges in depth as we proceed through this book. The intersection of these two worlds is not just a merger but a transformation that holds the promise of redefining healthcare in ways we are just beginning to understand.

By examining this fusion, we can prepare ourselves for a new healthcare era that carries immense promise but also warrants cautious optimism and ethical vigilance.

Chapter Eight

Types of AI in Healthcare

U nderstanding the types of AI technologies relevant to health-care allows us to grasp the breadth and scope of AI's transformative power in this sector. While AI's application in healthcare is vast and continually evolving, we can categorize its utility into several vital types:

Natural Language Processing (NLP):

Description:

- NLP focuses on the interaction between computers and human language. It helps machines understand, interpret, and respond to human text or speech.

Application in Healthcare:

- Medical transcription services convert voice-recorded medical reports into text.

- Sentiment analysis on patient feedback for hospital quality assessment.

- Automated chatbots for patient engagement and initial diagnosis.

Computer Vision:

Description:

- Computer Vision enables machines to interpret and make decisions based on visual data from the world, such as images or videos.

Application in Healthcare:

- Automated analysis of radiological images like X-rays, MRIs, and CT scans.

- Real-time monitoring of patients to detect falls or other emergencies.

- I am analyzing skin lesions and other visual symptoms via smartphones.

Predictive Analytics:

Description:

- Predictive analytics involves using statistical algorithms and machine learning techniques to identify the likelihood of future outcomes based on historical data.

Application in Healthcare:

- We are identifying high-risk patients for diseases like diabetes or cardiac issues.

- I am predicting patient admission rates for better resource allocation.

- We are analyzing the potential spread of infectious diseases.

Robotics:

Description:

- Robotics involves the creation of robots that can perform tasks in the real world, often mimicking human actions.

Application in Healthcare:

- Robotic-assisted surgery for enhanced precision and control.

- Rehabilitation robots to assist in physical therapy.

- Delivery robots for medicines and supplies within healthcare facilities.

Reinforcement Learning:

Description:

- Reinforcement Learning is a type of machine learning where an agent learns how to behave in an environment by performing actions and receiving rewards.

Application in Healthcare:

- Personalized treatment plans based on real-time patient data.

- Optimization of treatment policies in critical care units.

- Simulation-based medical training for healthcare professionals.

Expert Systems:

Description:

- Expert systems are computer programs that mimic the decision-making abilities of a human expert in specific domains.

Application in Healthcare:

- Diagnostic assistance for rare or complex conditions.

- Recommendations for drug interactions and side-effects.

- Decision support systems for healthcare management.

Understanding these types of AI technologies and their relevance to healthcare allows us to appreciate how AI can contribute to improving healthcare outcomes, reducing costs, and enhancing patient experiences.

By categorizing and detailing these technologies, this book aims to provide a structured lens through which healthcare providers, administrators, and patients can understand the transformative impact of AI in healthcare.

Chapter Nine

The Importance of AI in Healthcare

As we delve into the modern healthcare landscape, one thing becomes increasingly clear: Artificial Intelligence is no longer just a futuristic concept but an essential part of the medical ecosystem. Here, we discuss why AI is becoming indispensable in healthcare, focusing on three critical aspects: Efficiency, Accuracy, and Personalization.

Efficiency: Streamlining Administrative Tasks, Expediting Diagnosis

1. **Automating Routine Processes**: AI can handle administrative tasks that otherwise take up a substantial amount of healthcare providers' time, such as data entry, appointment scheduling, and billing. By automating these functions, doc-

tors and nurses can spend more time interacting with patients, offering a higher standard of care.

2. **Speeding Up Diagnosis**: Traditional diagnostic methods can be time-consuming. AI algorithms can analyze diagnostic tests, from blood reports to intricate MRI scans, in a fraction of the time it would take a human, often with equal or higher accuracy. This speed is crucial in time-sensitive situations, such as the early detection of life-threatening conditions.

Accuracy: Reducing Errors, Improving Patient Outcomes

1. **Error Reduction**: Medical errors, whether in diagnosis, medication prescription, or treatment administration, can have severe consequences. AI systems can cross-reference vast datasets to assist healthcare providers in making more accurate decisions, thereby reducing the margin for error.

2. **Data-Driven Decisions**: With AI, clinicians can make more informed decisions by analyzing past patient data, current health metrics, and even research studies, ultimately leading to improved patient outcomes.

Personalization: Tailoring Healthcare to Individual Needs

1. **Personalized Treatment Plans**: AI can analyze an indi-

vidual's medical history, genetic makeup, and lifestyle choices to recommend customized treatment plans. These custom-tailored plans can be more effective than one-size-fits-all approaches, leading to faster recovery times and improved quality of life.

2. **Chronic Disease Management**: For chronic conditions like diabetes, AI can help in monitoring patient metrics in real-time, adjusting medication levels, and even predicting potential flare-ups before they occur, allowing for preemptive action.

3. **Behavioral Health**: With natural language processing and machine learning algorithms, AI can monitor mental health indicators from text and voice inputs. This level of personalization can be pivotal in providing timely intervention and targeted mental health support.

AI is a beacon of innovation in an era when healthcare systems are under constant pressure due to growing populations, rising costs, and an increasing burden of chronic diseases. It promises to streamline operations, enhance the quality of care, and democratize access to healthcare services. But perhaps most importantly, AI heralds a shift from a one-size-fits-all healthcare model to personalized, patient-centric care. Doing so aligns closely with the ultimate goal of medicine: To provide the proper care for the right patient at the right time.

In conclusion, AI's increasing integration into healthcare is not just a trend but a significant advancement, promising a paradigm shift in how we approach medical care. Through efficiency, accuracy, and personalization, AI sets a new healthcare delivery standard.

Chapter Ten

Medical Imaging, Radiology, and Computer-Aided Diagnosis

The Triad of AI's Influence in Visual Medicine

A rtificial Intelligence (AI) 's impact is strongly felt in medical imaging, where it intersects with radiology and computer-aided diagnosis to create a robust triad that is revolutionizing healthcare. Here is an in-depth exploration of how these areas are interlinked and the unique contributions of AI in each:

Medical Imaging:

1. **Enhanced Imaging Techniques**: Advanced algorithms can optimize image acquisition parameters in real time, improving the quality of the images obtained via modalities like MRI, CT, and ultrasound.

2. **Image Reconstruction**: AI can accelerate the reconstruction of medical images, a process that traditionally could take a significant amount of time and computational power.

3. **Noise Reduction**: AI algorithms can reduce the noise in images, making it easier for radiologists to interpret them and potentially reducing the amount of radiation exposure for certain types of scans.

4. **Automated Annotation**: Machine learning models can automatically annotate and highlight areas of interest in medical images, saving precious time for medical professionals.

Radiology:

1. **Preliminary Diagnosis**: AI can assist radiologists by providing an initial diagnosis and flagging potential issues that require closer inspection.

2. **Workflow Optimization**: AI can streamline the workflow by prioritizing cases that appear more urgent, ensuring timely medical intervention.

3. **Interdisciplinary Collaboration**: AI-powered systems can bridge radiology and other specialties, providing a more integrated approach to patient care.

4. **Quality Assurance**: AI can help maintain the quality of radiological scans and reports, flagging inconsistencies or errors for human review.

Computer-Aided Diagnosis:

1. **Predictive Analytics**: Sophisticated algorithms can analyze historical and current data to predict the likelihood of various medical conditions, aiding in early detection and treatment planning.

2. **Treatment Recommendation**: Beyond diagnosis, some advanced systems can suggest treatment options based on the medical imaging data, clinical guidelines, and patient history.

3. **Second Opinion**: Computer-aided diagnosis systems can serve as a valuable second opinion for medical professionals, reinforcing their diagnostic decisions.

4. **Monitoring Progress**: These systems can also monitor treatment progress over time, providing quantitative metrics that can be used to adjust treatment plans as needed.

5. **Telemedicine Applications**: In areas where expert radiologists are scarce, computer-aided diagnosis can provide remote support, making quality healthcare more accessible.

Integrating AI into medical imaging, radiology, and computer-aided diagnosis is fundamentally changing the landscape of visual medicine. It promises faster, more accurate, and more personalized healthcare while introducing challenges that need thoughtful solutions, especially regarding ethical considerations and data integrity. The advancements in these domains exemplify the transformative power of AI in healthcare, offering a glimpse into a future where technology and medicine converge to improve human well-being.

Chapter Eleven

Drug Discovery

**Bridging the Gap Between Traditional Methods and
AI-Enabled Research**

T he drug discovery process is undergoing a seismic shift, thanks
to the inclusion of Artificial Intelligence (AI) in the research
pipeline. While traditional methods have their merits, AI-enabled research promises to make drug discovery faster, more accurate, and
cost-effective. Below is an analysis of how AI integrates with and augments traditional methods in drug discovery:

Traditional Methods in Drug Discovery:

1. **Target Identification**: The initial phase involves identifying biological targets involved in disease processes, like pro-
   teins or genes.

2. **High Throughput Screening**: Millions of compounds are
   tested against the identified targets to find potential drug

candidates.

3. **Animal Testing**: Promising compounds are tested for efficacy, toxicity, and pharmacokinetics.

4. **Clinical Trials**: After successful animal tests, the compounds enter multiple stages of human clinical trials.

5. **Regulatory Approval**: Drugs that pass all stages of clinical trials are submitted for regulatory approval, which is both time-consuming and expensive.

6. **Post-Marketing Surveillance**: Once approved, the drug is released into the market, but it continues to be monitored for long-term effects and safety.

AI-Enabled Research in Drug Discovery:

1. **AI in Target Identification**: Machine learning algorithms can analyze vast biomedical datasets to identify new drug targets more efficiently than traditional methods.

2. **In-silico Screening**: AI can predict how different compounds will behave and how likely they are to make an effective treatment, vastly reducing the number of compounds that need to be tested physically.

3. **Drug Repurposing**: AI can sift through existing drugs to see if any could be effective for new indications, potentially saving years of research.

4. **Predictive Modeling**: AI algorithms can predict how a drug

will interact with targets in the body, providing early indications of efficacy, toxicity, and potential side effects.

5. **Optimizing Clinical Trials**: AI can help design and monitor clinical trials, identify the most suitable candidates for trials and even predict patient outcomes.

6. **Automated Data Analysis**: During every phase of drug discovery, AI can automate the analysis of complex datasets, including everything from chemical structures to patient records.

7. **Regulatory Assistance**: NLP algorithms can assist in sorting through the labyrinth of regulatory documentation, making the approval process more streamlined.

Bridging the Gap:

1. **Speed**: AI technologies can significantly speed up drug discovery by automating repetitive tasks and analyzing data at a scale impossible for humans.

2. **Accuracy**: With machine learning algorithms, the accuracy of every step—from target identification to clinical trials—can be improved.

3. **Cost-effectiveness**: AI can potentially reduce the cost of drug discovery by eliminating less promising candidates earlier in the process and optimizing the remaining research pipeline.

4. **Ethical Benefits**: AI can reduce the need for animal test-

ing by providing more accurate simulations and predictive models.

5. **Interdisciplinary Synergy**: Combining traditional methods with AI enables a multidisciplinary approach, leveraging both strengths to create a more effective and efficient drug discovery process.

AI's impact on drug discovery is transformative, enhancing the capabilities of traditional methods and introducing new avenues of research. The blend of AI-enabled research and traditional methods holds immense promise for the future of drug discovery, potentially bringing life-saving drugs to market more quickly and affordably than ever before.

Chapter Twelve

Telemedicine

Uniting Remote Consultations with AI-Powered Diagnostic Tools

Telemedicine has already disrupted the traditional healthcare model by remotely enabling medical consultations and treatments. Adding Artificial Intelligence (AI) into the mix promises to further revolutionize medicine by enhancing remote consultations and equipping them with powerful diagnostic tools. Below, we explore the impact, benefits, and challenges of fusing telemedicine with AI technologies.

Telemedicine: The Base Technology

1. **Remote Consultations**: Doctors can consult patients through video conferencing, phone calls, or text, making healthcare more accessible for people living in remote or underserved areas.

2. **Telemonitoring**: Vital signs and other health metrics can be remotely monitored, effectively managing chronic conditions.

3. **E-Prescriptions**: Doctors can prescribe medications digitally, which is especially useful for routine refills or when immediate treatment is needed.

4. **Virtual Health Records**: Telemedicine platforms often maintain digital health records, making it easier for healthcare providers to collaborate and deliver comprehensive care.

AI-Powered Diagnosis Tools:

1. **Symptom Checkers**: AI-driven algorithms can evaluate patients' symptoms to suggest possible diagnoses, acting as a pre-consultation tool.

2. **Image Analysis**: AI can assist in interpreting medical images like X-rays or MRIs during a remote consultation, providing doctors with additional insights.

3. **Predictive Analytics**: AI can analyze a patient's medical history and current vitals to alert physicians to potential issues requiring immediate attention.

4. **Chatbots for Routine Queries**: AI-powered chatbots can handle routine questions and gather preliminary patient data before the consultation, freeing healthcare providers to focus on more complex tasks.

5. **Natural Language Processing**: Advanced NLP algorithms

can convert spoken content during consultations into structured data, making it easier to maintain accurate medical records.

Bringing Them Together: Benefits and Challenges

Benefits:

1. **Accessibility**: AI can magnify the reach of telemedicine, making specialized consultations accessible even in remote regions.

2. **Efficiency**: AI-powered tools can streamline the diagnostic and treatment process, enabling healthcare providers to handle more cases more accurately.

3. **Cost-Effectiveness**: Automating routine tasks and analytics can significantly lower the cost of providing quality healthcare.

4. **Data-Driven Decisions**: The union of AI and telemedicine provides a rich data set that can be analyzed for insights into patient care and treatment effectiveness.

Challenges:

1. **Data Security**: Integrating AI into telemedicine introduces new vulnerabilities that need robust cybersecurity measures.

2. **Regulatory Compliance**: Both telemedicine and AI must navigate a complex landscape of medical regulations and data protection laws.

3. **Ethical Concerns**: Patient consent, data ownership, and AI biases require careful consideration to ensure ethical medical practice.

4. **Quality of Care**: Ensuring that the quality of healthcare provided through AI-augmented telemedicine meets or exceeds traditional methods is crucial for widespread adoption.

5. **Technical Limitations**: Both telemedicine and AI require a certain level of technological infrastructure, which may be lacking in some regions.

The integration of AI into telemedicine has the potential to reshape the healthcare industry dramatically. It offers a promising route to more accessible, efficient, and personalized healthcare, though its challenges must be addressed thoughtfully. As both technologies continue to evolve, the synergy between them could become a cornerstone of the next generation of healthcare delivery.

Chapter Thirteen

Predictive Analytics in Healthcare

From Risk Assessment to Health Outcomes Prediction

A s healthcare evolves into a more data-centric field, predictive analytics is increasingly becoming vital for clinicians, administrators, and patients. By analyzing patterns in large sets of healthcare data, predictive analytics aims to forecast patient risk, assess potential outcomes, and inform treatment options. This approach has tremendous implications for risk assessment and the prediction of health outcomes. Below is a detailed examination of how predictive analytics serves these functions.

Predictive Analytics: An Overview

1. **Data Sources**: From Electronic Health Records (EHRs) to wearable devices, numerous sources feed into predictive analytics models.

2. **Technological Framework**: Various forms of AI, including machine learning and neural networks, power these analytics tools.

3. **Interdisciplinary Approach**: Predictive analytics often combines expertise from healthcare, data science, statistics, and information technology to build robust predictive models.

Risk Assessment:

1. **Identification of High-Risk Patients**: By analyzing historical data, predictive analytics can identify patients at high risk for various conditions, such as diabetes, cardiovascular diseases, or readmissions.

2. **Early Warning Systems**: In a hospital setting, predictive analytics can provide early warnings for severe conditions like sepsis or acute kidney injury, allowing timely interventions.

3. **Resource Allocation**: Knowing which patients are at higher risk enables better allocation of resources, such as targeted follow-ups and tailored care plans.

4. **Insurance Premium Calculation**: Predictive analytics can also be used to more accurately assess the risk associated with

individual patients, thereby helping insurance companies set premiums.

Health Outcomes Prediction:

1. **Treatment Optimization**: Predictive models can forecast how different patient demographics will respond to various treatments, aiding clinicians in making more personalized decisions.

2. **Surgery Success Rate**: Predictive analytics can estimate the likely success and potential complications of surgical procedures based on the patient's history and current health status.

3. **Chronic Disease Management**: For chronic conditions like diabetes or heart disease, predictive analytics can anticipate potential flare-ups or complications, helping doctors and patients manage the condition more effectively.

4. **Mortality Prediction**: In critical care settings, analytics tools can predict patient mortality risks, which is crucial for making end-of-life care decisions.

Advantages and Challenges:

Advantages:

1. **Personalized Medicine**: Predictive analytics paves the way for more personalized and effective treatments.

2. **Cost-Reduction**: Early identification of high-risk patients can result in timely interventions, reducing the overall cost of care.

3. **Improved Quality of Care**: More accurate predictions mean better care, improved patient outcomes, and enhanced healthcare delivery.

Challenges:

1. **Data Privacy and Security**: With the increased use of data comes the increased risk of data breaches or unauthorized access.

2. **Ethical Concerns**: Questions about data ownership, consent, and potential bias in predictive models are ongoing challenges.

3. **Interoperability**: Effective predictive analytics requires seamless data integration from multiple sources, often hindered by interoperability between EHR systems.

4. **Model Transparency**: Ensuring clinicians understand how predictive models arrive at conclusions is crucial for trust and accountability.

Predictive analytics offers a powerful new approach to healthcare, especially in risk assessment and health outcomes prediction. While there are challenges to overcome, the benefits of personalized treatment and resource optimization are transformative, heralding a new era in data-driven healthcare.

Chapter Fourteen

EHR and Administrative Tasks

The Role of AI in Automating Data Entry and Natural Language Processing

E lectronic Health Records (EHRs) have become indispensable for storing vast amounts of patient information in modern healthcare. However, they also present several challenges, such as administrative burdens and the time-consuming nature of manual data entry. Artificial Intelligence (AI), particularly through Natural Language Processing (NLP), offers promising solutions for these challenges. Below, we delve into how AI revolutionizes EHR management and administrative tasks.

EHR and Administrative Challenges:

1. **Manual Data Entry**: Physicians and healthcare staff often spend a disproportionate amount of time entering data into EHRs, which can detract from patient care.

2. **Data Retrieval**: Finding relevant information within extensive EHRs can be cumbersome and time-consuming.

3. **Error Rates**: Manual data entry increases the likelihood of errors, significantly affecting patient care.

4. **Interoperability**: Different healthcare providers often use disparate EHR systems, complicating data sharing and integration.

Automating Data Entry:

1. **Voice Recognition**: Advanced voice recognition software can convert spoken medical notes into text, significantly reducing the time required for data entry.

2. **Image Recognition**: Machine learning algorithms can automatically extract relevant information from medical images and populate EHRs.

3. **IoT Devices**: Wearables and other medical devices can directly feed data into EHRs, eliminating manual entry for vitals and other metrics.

4. **Template-based Solutions**: AI algorithms can recognize patterns and suggest templates for common medical records,

making data entry more streamlined.

Natural Language Processing (NLP):

1. **Semantic Search**: NLP can enable semantic search within EHRs, making it easier for healthcare providers to find relevant information.

2. **Clinical Decision Support**: By understanding the context of the medical notes, NLP can provide real-time recommendations or alerts, assisting clinicians in making informed decisions.

3. **Coding and Billing**: NLP can automatically identify billing codes based on the medical procedures and diagnoses documented in the EHR, reducing administrative load and errors.

4. **Sentiment Analysis**: Analyzing patient feedback or comments can help gauge patient satisfaction and identify areas for improvement.

The Way Forward:

Advantages:

1. **Efficiency**: Automation and NLP significantly reduce the time healthcare providers must spend on administrative tasks, allowing them to focus more on patient care.

2. **Accuracy**: AI algorithms can significantly reduce errors in data entry and retrieval, leading to safer and more effective healthcare.

3. **Compliance**: Automated systems can be designed to adhere to regulatory standards, ensuring that EHRs meet legal requirements.

Challenges:

1. **Data Security**: Automation increases the risk of data breaches and must be managed with robust cybersecurity measures.

2. **Adoption Barriers**: Resistance to new technologies from healthcare staff can slow the adoption of automated systems.

3. **Cost**: The initial investment in AI and automation technologies can be high, though long-term benefits will likely offset them.

4. **Algorithmic Bias**: Care must be taken to ensure that NLP algorithms are designed and trained in a way that avoids bias.

AI, particularly NLP, has the potential to dramatically improve the efficiency and accuracy of EHRs and administrative tasks in healthcare. While challenges remain, the benefits of time saved, reduced errors, and improved patient care are considerable, making this an area ripe for continued innovation and adoption.

Chapter Fifteen

Emerging Trends in Healthcare

A Focus on Robot-Assisted Surgery, Current Technologies, and Future Prospects

T he healthcare landscape continuously evolves, with technology playing an increasingly pivotal role. One of the most transformative emerging trends is the rise of robot-assisted surgery, offering groundbreaking opportunities and challenges. This section provides an exhaustive overview of current technologies and ponders the prospects in this dynamic arena.

Robot-Assisted Surgery:

1. **What is Robot-Assisted Surgery?**: An introduction to robot-assisted surgical systems, including their core components and functionalities.

2. **Benefits and Drawbacks**: A balanced look at the advantages, such as precision and minimally invasive procedures, and the drawbacks, like cost and accessibility.

3. **Case Studies**: Real-world examples showcasing the impact of robot-assisted surgeries in specialties like urology, orthopedics, and cardiothoracic surgery.

4. **Regulatory Landscape**: Examining FDA approvals, quality controls, and other regulatory factors influencing robot-assisted surgery.

Current Technologies:

1. **Da Vinci Surgical System**: The most widely used robot-assisted system, capabilities, and application areas.

2. **Senhance Surgical System**: A newer entrant focusing on haptic feedback and eye-tracking technology.

3. **RAS Devices in Imaging**: How robots aid imaging processes, including biopsy procedures and intricate diagnostics.

4. **Virtual Reality in Pre-Operative Planning**: VR simulates surgeries for educational and planning purposes.

Future Prospects:

1. **AI-Enhanced Robotics**: Integrating Artificial Intelligence with robot-assisted surgery for predictive analytics and

real-time decision-making.

2. **Tele-Surgery**: The possibility of surgeons operating remotely, potentially providing high-quality surgical care to underserved regions.

3. **Affordability and Accessibility**: Innovations that aim to make robot-assisted surgical systems more affordable and accessible to healthcare providers globally.

4. **Ethical and Social Considerations**: As robot-assisted surgery becomes more advanced, what ethical dilemmas and social implications must we grapple with?

Conclusions and the Path Forward:

Advantages:

1. **Precision and Control**: Robot-assisted surgery allows for unparalleled precision, making complex surgeries safer and more effective.

2. **Minimally Invasive Procedures**: Many robot-assisted surgeries can be done through small incisions, reducing recovery time and minimizing complications.

Challenges:

1. **High Costs**: The costs of procuring and maintaining ro-

botic surgical systems can be prohibitively high for many healthcare institutions.

2. **Skills Gap**: Surgeons and medical staff need specialized training to operate these systems, creating a learning curve.

3. **Ethical Concerns**: The evolving role of robots in healthcare introduces a host of ethical considerations, from job displacement to patient consent.

Emerging trends like robot-assisted surgery are irrevocably changing the face of healthcare, introducing remarkable capabilities and intricate challenges. As technology advances, it becomes crucial to address these issues comprehensively to ensure that the healthcare industry leverages these innovations for patient care.

Chapter Sixteen

Wearable Health Tech

A Deep Dive into Monitoring Devices and Data Analysis

I n the rapidly evolving world of healthcare technology, wearables have emerged as a significant game-changer. They offer the potential for continuous health monitoring and data collection, substantially impacting patient care and preventive medicine. This section will provide a comprehensive look at wearable health technology, focusing on monitoring devices and the critical role of data analysis.

Wearable Health Monitoring Devices:

1. **Types of Devices**: An overview of different wearables, from fitness trackers and smartwatches to specialized medical devices like ECG monitors and glucose sensors.

2. **Functionality**: A detailed look at what these devices can monitor, including vital signs like heart rate, blood pressure, blood oxygen levels, sleep quality and physical activity.

3. **User Experience**: How wearables are designed for user comfort, battery life, and ease of use, along with features like alerts and notifications.

4. **Data Security and Privacy**: The encryption and security measures in place to protect user data and the legal and ethical considerations surrounding data ownership and sharing.

Data Analysis:

1. **Data Aggregation**: How data from wearable devices is aggregated for analysis, either through smartphone apps or dedicated healthcare platforms.

2. **Machine Learning Algorithms**: How machine learning and other advanced analytics techniques are employed to interpret the raw data, identify patterns, and make predictions.

3. **Clinical Applications**: The use of wearable data in clinical settings for diagnosis, treatment planning, and monitoring of chronic conditions like diabetes and cardiovascular diseases.

4. **Public Health Impact**: How aggregated data from wearables can be used for more significant public health initiatives, including epidemiological studies and population health management.

The Future Landscape:

1. **Integration with Traditional Healthcare**: How wearable tech is increasingly integrated into mainstream healthcare, including EHRs and telemedicine platforms.

2. **Next-Generation Wearables**: The next generation might include more advanced sensors, better battery life, and real-time analysis capabilities.

3. **Ethical and Regulatory Considerations**: Ongoing challenges in data privacy, informed consent, and potential inequalities in access to these advanced technologies exist.

Conclusion:

Advantages:

1. **Preventive Medicine**: Wearables allow for real-time monitoring, which can help in early diagnosis and preventive interventions, reducing the overall healthcare burden.

2. **Personalization**: The detailed data gathered can be used to tailor healthcare and lifestyle interventions to individual needs, offering a more personalized approach to health and well-being.

Challenges:

1. **Data Overload**: The sheer volume of data generated can be overwhelming for healthcare providers and may require specialized skills for meaningful interpretation.

2. **Affordability and Accessibility**: High costs and the need for smartphones or other connected devices could limit the accessibility of wearable health tech.

Wearable health tech represents a revolutionary shift in healthcare, offering many new opportunities and challenges. With the capability to continuously monitor health metrics, these devices are moving us closer to a future of personalized, data-driven healthcare. However, several challenges around data management, security, and ethics must be addressed to fully realize this potential.

Chapter Seventeen

Genomic Medicine

Unravelling Genome Sequencing for Personalized Treatment

The advent of genomic medicine heralds a new era in healthcare, promising a highly personalized approach to diagnosis and treatment. By harnessing the power of genome sequencing, this evolving field seeks to understand the genetic basis of diseases, paving the way for targeted therapies and more effective health management. This section delves into the complexities and potential of genomic medicine, focusing on genome sequencing and personalized treatment plans.

Genome Sequencing:

1. **What is Genome Sequencing?**: A primer on the technolo-

gies and methodologies involved in sequencing the human genome, such as Next-Generation Sequencing (NGS) and Whole Genome Sequencing (WGS).

2. **Applications in Healthcare**: An overview of how genome sequencing is used in clinical settings to diagnose rare diseases, identify mutations, and assess individual risks for specific conditions.

3. **Cost and Accessibility**: An analysis of the declining cost of genome sequencing and how it impacts accessibility for the general population.

4. **Ethical and Privacy Concerns**: Addressing questions around data ownership, consent, and the ethical implications of access to one's genetic makeup.

Personalized Treatment:

1. **Targeted Therapies**: A look at how genomic information can guide the choice of drugs and treatments most likely effective for individual patients.

2. **Pharmacogenomics**: Understanding how a person's genetic makeup can affect their response to drugs, leading to personalized dosages and minimizing adverse reactions.

3. **Personalized Prevention Plans**: How genomic data can be used to create preventive healthcare strategies tailored to individual genetic profiles.

4. **Integration with EHR**: The challenges and opportunities

in integrating genomic data into Electronic Health Records for a holistic view of patient health.

The Future of Genomic Medicine:

1. **Population-Scale Genomics**: The implications and opportunities of sequencing genomes on a population scale for research and public health.

2. **AI and Genomics**: How artificial intelligence algorithms can analyze vast genomic datasets to uncover new disease markers, drug targets, and treatment pathways.

3. **Regulatory Landscape**: An overview of current regulations governing the use of genomic data in healthcare and what needs to evolve as the technology matures.

Conclusion:

Advantages:

1. **Precision Medicine**: Genomic medicine allows for a more accurate diagnosis and treatment, significantly improving patient outcomes.

2. **Proactive Healthcare**: The potential for early identification of genetic risks allows for proactive measures, reducing the incidence and impact of many diseases.

Challenges:

1. **Data Complexity**: The enormous amount of data generated by genome sequencing requires sophisticated analysis and interpretation, often demanding specialized expertise.

2. **Ethical Dilemmas**: Data privacy, discrimination based on genetic information, and informed consent continue to pose challenges.

Genomic medicine is redefining our understanding of healthcare, moving us from a one-size-fits-all approach to a personalized paradigm. The potential benefits are vast, from targeted treatments to preventive health strategies tailored to an individual's genetic makeup. However, the field has challenges, especially concerning data management, ethics, and inclusivity. As genome sequencing becomes more affordable and accessible, the onus is on healthcare providers, regulators, and society to ensure this powerful technology is used responsibly and equitably.

Chapter Eighteen

AI in Mental Health

Chatbots, Online Therapy, and Monitoring Mental Health Metrics

The landscape of mental healthcare is undergoing a dramatic transformation spurred by the advent of artificial intelligence. Whether through chatbots offering immediate emotional support or advanced algorithms analyzing mental health metrics, AI is making mental healthcare more accessible, efficient, and personalized. This section provides a comprehensive analysis of the role of AI in mental health, focusing on chatbots, online therapy, and monitoring mental health metrics.

Chatbots and Online Therapy:

1. **What are Mental Health Chatbots?**: An introduction to

AI-driven chatbots specifically designed for mental health support, including their underlying technologies and critical features.

2. **Efficacy and Limitations**: A critical evaluation of how effective chatbots and online therapy platforms are compared to traditional forms of therapy.

3. **User Privacy and Data Security**: An exploration of how these platforms ensure user confidentiality and what ethical considerations are in place regarding data storage and sharing.

4. **Regulatory Landscape**: Current regulations governing the use of AI in mental health, including licensure of online therapists and oversight of chatbot algorithms.

Monitoring Mental Health Metrics:

1. **Types of Metrics**: A rundown of the various mental health metrics that can be monitored, from mood and emotion tracking to biometrics like heart rate variability.

2. **AI-Enabled Analysis**: How machine learning and data analytics interpret these metrics, leading to actionable insights for clinicians or self-care strategies for individuals.

3. **Integration with Traditional Therapy**: The challenges and opportunities of incorporating AI-generated metrics into standard therapeutic practices.

4. **Ethical Considerations**: Discussion around the ethics of

continuous mental health monitoring, including issues of
consent and potential for data misuse.

The Future of AI in Mental Health:

1. **Telepsychiatry and AI**: The potential for AI to augment
   telepsychiatry, making remote mental healthcare more effective and widely accessible.

2. **Natural Language Processing (NLP)**: Future developments in NLP that could make mental health chatbots more
   responsive and accurate.

3. **Accessibility and Equity**: How AI could help bridge the
   gap in mental health services for underserved populations.

Conclusion:

Advantages:

1. **Immediate Support**: AI-enabled platforms can provide
   quick, round-the-clock assistance, offering a crucial support
   network for those who may not have direct access to human
   therapists.

2. **Data-Driven Insights**: Using metrics and data analysis allows for a more nuanced understanding of an individual's
   mental health, which can be invaluable in creating personalized treatment plans.

Challenges:

1. **Quality of Care**: The need to ensure that AI-driven mental health solutions meet the same quality and efficacy standards as traditional therapeutic methods.

2. **Ethical and Privacy Concerns**: Ongoing issues related to data security, patient confidentiality, and informed consent.

AI is steadily reshaping the mental healthcare landscape, offering tools that can complement and sometimes even substitute traditional therapeutic practices. The prospects are exciting, from chatbots for immediate support to AI-driven analytics for a more personalized approach to treatment. However, to fully leverage these advancements, a stringent focus on efficacy, ethics, and data security will be essential as technology evolves.

Chapter Nineteen

Future Possibilities of AI in Healthcare

Personalized Medicine, Tailoring Individual Treatments, and the Potential for Breakthroughs

A s artificial intelligence advances at an unprecedented pace, its implications for healthcare are becoming increasingly profound. The future promises even more revolutionary changes, offering a glimpse into a world where healthcare is profoundly personalized, treatments are fine-tuned to the individual, and medical breakthroughs occur rapidly. This section delves into these exciting possibilities, painting a picture of the future.

Personalized Medicine:

1. **Advanced Diagnostics**: The potential for AI algorithms to analyze an individual's genetic makeup, lifestyle data, and even social determinants of health to diagnose conditions more accurately and earlier.

2. **Treatment Plans**: How AI could leverage vast amounts of data to formulate treatment plans tailored to individual patient's unique genetic and biochemical makeup.

3. **Personalized Nutrition and Exercise**: The possibility of AI-powered platforms that offer customized nutrition and exercise plans based on individual health metrics and medical history.

4. **Precision Drug Development**: How AI could accelerate the development of new drugs tailored to specific genetic profiles, bypassing the "one-size-fits-all" approach.

AI in Tailoring Individual Treatments:

1. **Dynamic Treatment Adaptation**: The potential for real-time adjustment of treatment plans based on continuously monitored health metrics, ensuring optimal efficacy and minimizing side effects.

2. **Patient Monitoring**: How wearable devices and other sensors could feed data into AI algorithms, which then adapt treatment plans without the need for frequent doctor visits.

3. **Virtual Health Assistants**: The development of advanced AI agents capable of guiding patients through their treat-

ment plans, providing reminders, and even alerting healthcare providers in an emergency.

Potential for Breakthroughs:

1. **AI in Research**: The promise of AI in speeding up the pace
   of medical research, from initial hypothesis generation to
   clinical trials and commercialization.

2. **Uncovering Unknown Pathways**: How AI could analyze
   vast datasets to find previously unknown biological pathways and mechanisms of disease, leading to entirely new
   treatment categories.

3. **Revolutionizing Mental Health**: The role AI could play
   in fundamentally transforming mental healthcare through
   predictive analytics, immediate support through chatbots,
   and more.

Conclusion:

Advantages:

1. **Speed and Efficiency**: AI has the potential to significantly
   speed up both diagnosis and the development of new treatments, making healthcare more efficient.

2. **Inclusivity and Access**: AI-powered healthcare solutions
   could be more easily scaled, bringing high-quality healthcare

to underserved communities worldwide.

Challenges:

1. **Ethical and Regulatory Concerns**: As AI takes on an ever-greater role in healthcare, new ethical and regulatory frameworks must be established to ensure patient safety and privacy.

2. **Data Integrity and Security**: The large amounts of data required for AI to function effectively in healthcare increase the risk of data breaches and other security concerns.

The potential of AI to revolutionize healthcare is beyond exciting. The future holds the promise of a healthcare system that is more efficient, effective and far more personalized. Whether through fine-tuned treatment plans, accelerated drug discovery, or groundbreaking research, AI makes a significant impact on how healthcare is delivered and experienced. As we stand on the cusp of this new era, the challenges are many, but the opportunities are truly boundless.

Chapter Twenty

Future Possibilities of AI in Healthcare

Personalized Medicine, Tailoring Individual Treatments, and the Potential for Breakthroughs

A s artificial intelligence advances at an unprecedented pace, its implications for healthcare are becoming increasingly profound. The future promises even more revolutionary changes, offering a glimpse into a world where healthcare is profoundly personalized, treatments are fine-tuned to the individual, and medical breakthroughs occur rapidly. This section delves into these exciting possibilities, painting a picture of the future.

Personalized Medicine:

1. **Advanced Diagnostics**: The potential for AI algorithms to analyze an individual's genetic makeup, lifestyle data, and even social determinants of health to diagnose conditions more accurately and earlier.

2. **Treatment Plans**: How AI could leverage vast amounts of data to formulate treatment plans tailored to individual patient's unique genetic and biochemical makeup.

3. **Personalized Nutrition and Exercise**: The possibility of AI-powered platforms that offer customized nutrition and exercise plans based on individual health metrics and medical history.

4. **Precision Drug Development**: How AI could accelerate the development of new drugs tailored to specific genetic profiles, bypassing the "one-size-fits-all" approach.

AI in Tailoring Individual Treatments:

1. **Dynamic Treatment Adaptation**: The potential for real-time adjustment of treatment plans based on continuously monitored health metrics, ensuring optimal efficacy and minimizing side effects.

2. **Patient Monitoring**: How wearable devices and other sensors could feed data into AI algorithms, which then adapt treatment plans without the need for frequent doctor visits.

3. **Virtual Health Assistants**: The development of advanced AI agents capable of guiding patients through their treat-

ment plans, providing reminders, and even alerting healthcare providers in an emergency.

Potential for Breakthroughs:

1. **AI in Research**: The promise of AI in speeding up the pace
   of medical research, from initial hypothesis generation to
   clinical trials and commercialization.

2. **Uncovering Unknown Pathways**: How AI could analyze
   vast datasets to find previously unknown biological pathways and mechanisms of disease, leading to entirely new
   treatment categories.

3. **Revolutionizing Mental Health**: The role AI could play
   in fundamentally transforming mental healthcare through
   predictive analytics, immediate support through chatbots,
   and more.

Conclusion:

Advantages:

1. **Speed and Efficiency**: AI has the potential to significantly
   speed up both diagnosis and the development of new treatments, making healthcare more efficient.

2. **Inclusivity and Access**: AI-powered healthcare solutions
   could be more easily scaled, bringing high-quality healthcare

to underserved communities worldwide.

Challenges:

1. **Ethical and Regulatory Concerns**: As AI takes on an ever-greater role in healthcare, new ethical and regulatory frameworks must be established to ensure patient safety and privacy.

2. **Data Integrity and Security**: The large amounts of data required for AI to function effectively in healthcare increase the risk of data breaches and other security concerns.

The potential of AI to revolutionize healthcare is beyond exciting. The future holds the promise of a healthcare system that is more efficient, effective and far more personalized. Whether through fine-tuned treatment plans, accelerated drug discovery, or groundbreaking research, AI makes a significant impact on how healthcare is delivered and experienced. As we stand on the cusp of this new era, the challenges are many, but the opportunities are truly boundless.

Chapter
Twenty-One

AI in Global
Health

Remote Monitoring and Treatment, Epidemic Prediction, and Control

T he impact of Artificial Intelligence (AI) on healthcare is not restricted to the walls of hospitals or the confines of specific countries. It has the transformative potential to extend its reach globally, revolutionizing healthcare access, monitoring, and treatment in diverse settings. This is particularly significant for global health challenges, such as remote healthcare delivery, epidemic prediction, and control. This section will explore the emerging trends and future possibilities of AI's role in global health.

Remote Monitoring and Treatment:

1. **Telehealth Systems**: How AI can bolster telehealth initiatives, providing high-quality healthcare consultations for people in remote and underserved areas.

2. **Remote Patient Monitoring**: The use of AI in wearable devices and sensors to monitor vital signs, disease symptoms, and medication adherence from afar.

3. **AI-Driven Decision Support**: How AI algorithms can assist healthcare providers in remote areas with diagnosis and treatment planning, even without the immediate availability of specialists.

4. **Automated Pharmacies and Medicine Dispensers**: The use of AI to manage medication distribution in areas that lack sufficient healthcare infrastructure.

Epidemic Prediction and Control:

1. **Predictive Modeling**: The role of AI in predicting outbreaks by analyzing diverse datasets, including climate data, population density, and social media posts.

2. **Resource Allocation**: AI algorithms that can optimize the distribution of healthcare resources, such as vaccines and medical supplies, based on real-time needs.

3. **Contact Tracing and Quarantine Management**: How AI can streamline and improve the efficiency of contact tracing

efforts and enforce quarantine measures.

4. **Public Health Communication**: The use of Natural Language Processing (NLP) in chatbots and automated systems to disseminate accurate information about epidemics and recommended preventive measures.

Conclusion:

Advantages:

1. **Scale and Reach**: AI technologies can be scaled globally, providing opportunities to address systemic healthcare disparities and bring quality healthcare to remote regions.

2. **Proactive Intervention**: AI's predictive capabilities can facilitate more aggressive approaches, allowing for timely interventions that could save lives and resources.

Challenges:

1. **Data Privacy and Security**: The global scale of these solutions intensifies the ethical and legal concerns around data privacy and security.

2. **Cultural and Linguistic Barriers**: The effectiveness of AI solutions in a global context will depend on their ability to overcome cultural and linguistic barriers, requiring context-sensitive algorithms and localized interfaces.

The promise of AI in global health is immense. It has the potential to flatten disparities in healthcare access and quality, both within and between countries. While AI can't replace the human touch in healthcare, its vast analytical capabilities can make it a powerful ally in the fight against global health challenges. As we navigate the complexities of implementing AI globally, the key will be to balance technological possibilities with ethical imperatives.

Chapter Twenty-Two

Speculative Technologies

Brain-Computer Interfaces, AI in Longevity Research

In speculative technologies, the intersection of Artificial Intelligence (AI) with healthcare takes on an almost science-fiction quality. From brain-computer interfaces that could potentially allow direct communication between machines and the human brain to AI-driven longevity research aiming to extend human life, these speculative technologies give us a glimpse into what the far future of healthcare might look like. This section will delve into these exciting yet ethically complex frontiers.

Brain-Computer Interfaces:

1. **Direct Neural Control**: The potential for brain-computer interfaces to allow individuals, particularly those with mo-

bility impairments, to control prosthetics or computers directly through neural signals.

2. **Cognitive Enhancement**: The ethical and philosophical implications of using brain-computer interfaces for enhancing human cognition and abilities.

3. **Mental Health Applications**: How these interfaces could potentially diagnose and treat mental health conditions by interacting directly with neural pathways.

4. **Ethical Concerns**: Privacy, informed consent, and the potential for misuse, especially in contexts like law enforcement or authoritarian regimes.

AI in Longevity Research:

1. **Genomic Analysis**: The role of AI in analyzing genetic factors that contribute to aging and lifespan, aiming to identify targets for anti-aging interventions.

2. **Drug Discovery**: How AI could accelerate the identification and testing of compounds extending lifespan or improving health in old age.

3. **Data-Driven Lifestyle Recommendations**: AI's potential to analyze large datasets to offer personalized recommendations for lifestyle changes aimed at extending healthy lifespan.

4. **Ethical Questions**: The social and ethical considerations of extending human lifespan, including issues of resource

allocation, social inequality, and the moral implications of "defeating death."

Conclusion:

Advantages:

1. **Unlocking New Frontiers**: These speculative technologies could open up new possibilities for healthcare and human experience, from mitigating severe disabilities to extending healthy human life.

2. **Precision and Personalization**: The precision and personalization that could be achieved with these technologies are unprecedented, potentially revolutionizing how healthcare is delivered.

Challenges:

1. **Ethical Quandaries**: The advancements come with significant ethical questions that society must grapple with, including consent, fairness, and the very definition of what it means to be human.

2. **Regulatory Hurdles**: Given the groundbreaking nature of these technologies, existing regulatory frameworks may be inadequate, requiring the development of new laws and ethical guidelines.

As we look to the future, speculative technologies like brain-computer interfaces and AI in longevity research present thrilling opportunities and daunting challenges. These technologies push the boundaries of what is currently possible, inviting us to reimagine the future of healthcare and human potential. Yet, they also raise complex ethical questions that require thoughtful deliberation and societal consensus. As we stand on the precipice of these new frontiers, the need for careful ethical and regulatory guidance has never been greater.

Chapter Twenty-Three

Challenges and Future Prospects

Interoperability, Data Exchange Standards, Future Solutions

A s the healthcare industry braces for a seismic shift propelled by Artificial Intelligence (AI), challenges that require meticulous planning and solutions emerge. Interoperability and data exchange standards are among the key obstacles that stand in the way of a fully integrated, AI-augmented healthcare landscape. In this section, we delve into these challenges and explore possible solutions that could define the future of healthcare.

Interoperability:

1. **System Compatibility**: One of the significant challenges is ensuring that different AI tools and healthcare databases are compatible, allowing for smooth data flow and system interactions.

2. **Legacy Systems**: The presence of older, less flexible systems in many healthcare institutions complicates the adoption of new AI technologies.

3. **Multi-vendor Environments**: With multiple vendors supplying different components of the healthcare system, achieving seamless interoperability becomes even more challenging.

4. **Legal Barriers**: Data-sharing agreements and regulations can often hinder the full interoperability between systems, particularly across international borders.

Data Exchange Standards:

1. **Standardization**: The lack of universal data formatting and exchange standards in healthcare system components is a significant obstacle to effective data sharing.

2. **Quality and Consistency**: Varying quality and consistency of healthcare data can undermine the effectiveness of AI algorithms, which require high-quality, standardized data to function optimally.

3. **Privacy and Security**: Ensuring the secure and ethical handling of sensitive patient data is necessary, and the standards

are still under development.

Future Solutions:

1. **Unified Standards**: Developing and adopting unified data exchange standards could dramatically improve interoperability.

2. **Open APIs**: Open Application Programming Interfaces (APIs) could allow for greater flexibility and integration between disparate systems.

3. **Blockchain Technology**: Utilizing blockchain for secure, tamper-proof data exchange systems could address many privacy and security concerns.

4. **Public-Private Partnerships**: Collaborations between government agencies, healthcare providers, and tech companies can accelerate the development of interoperable systems and data exchange standards.

Conclusion:

Advantages:

1. **Seamless Healthcare Delivery**: Achieving full interoperability and standardized data exchange would facilitate more effective and efficient healthcare delivery.

2. **Innovation**: Standardization could spur innovation by making it easier for startups and smaller companies to enter the space, knowing they can integrate their solutions into existing systems.

Challenges:

1. **Complexity**: The sheer complexity of healthcare systems and their many components makes achieving full interoperability daunting.

2. **Regulatory Landscape**: The evolving regulatory landscape will continue to pose challenges for data sharing and system compatibility.

As the integration of AI into healthcare progresses, overcoming challenges related to interoperability and data exchange standards becomes critical. By addressing these issues, we can unlock a future where AI enhances individual aspects of healthcare and becomes integrated into a seamlessly functioning, efficient, and patient-centric system. While the challenges are significant, the potential rewards—improved patient outcomes, more efficient healthcare delivery, and innovations we can't imagine—are too great to ignore.

Chapter
Twenty-Four

Regulatory
Landscape

FDA Approval for AI in Medicine, Ethical Guidelines

Incorporating Artificial Intelligence (AI) into healthcare is a technological challenge and a regulatory one. Ensuring AI technologies' safety, efficacy, and ethical application requires a robust framework of guidelines and approvals. This section dissects the regulatory landscape, including the U.S. Food and Drug Administration's (FDA) role and the ethical considerations that must guide AI's application in healthcare.

FDA Approval for AI in Medicine:

1. **Pre-market Approval (PMA)**: Any new AI tool intend-

ed for medical use must undergo a rigorous PMA process, where its safety and effectiveness are thoroughly evaluated.

2. **De Novo Classification**: For novel devices without a predicate, a 'De Novo' request can be made to classify the device into Class I or II, determining the level of control required to assure safety and effectiveness.

3. **510(k) Clearance**: A 510(k) premarket notification is usually sufficient for devices similar to existing approved devices. Manufacturers must show that their product is "substantially equivalent" to an already approved device.

4. **Post-market Surveillance**: FDA approval isn't the end of the road. AI systems must undergo ongoing monitoring to ensure they continue to meet safety and effectiveness criteria.

5. **Real-World Evidence**: The FDA increasingly considers real-world evidence in its evaluations, requiring rigorous post-market studies that prove an AI tool's value in clinical settings.

Ethical Guidelines:

1. **Transparency**: Patients and healthcare providers should be informed when an AI system is involved in their care, along with the limitations and capabilities of that system.

2. **Informed Consent**: Users should give explicit consent for the use of AI in their healthcare, especially for sensitive applications like genetic testing or mental health assessments.

3. **Data Privacy**: AI applications must adhere to healthcare data privacy regulations, like HIPAA in the United States, ensuring that patient data is secure and confidential.

4. **Bias and Fairness**: Efforts must be made to minimize algorithmic bias that could perpetuate healthcare inequalities. AI systems should be trained on diverse datasets and regularly audited for fairness.

5. **Accountability**: There should be clear guidelines on accountability in cases where AI systems make errors or produce undesirable outcomes, including the potential for legal ramifications.

Conclusion:

Advantages:

1. **Ensured Safety**: A thorough FDA approval process means that any AI technology used in healthcare has been rigorously tested for safety and effectiveness.

2. **Ethical Assurance**: Well-defined ethical guidelines ensure that AI applications respect patient rights and social norms.

Challenges:

1. **Regulatory Hurdles**: Obtaining FDA approval is a long, expensive process that can slow the deployment of poten-

tially life-saving technologies.

2. **Ethical Complexity**: The ethical implications of using AI in healthcare are often complex and still the subject of ongoing debate.

The regulatory landscape for AI in healthcare is complex but necessary to ensure the safe and ethical deployment of new technologies. As AI continues to evolve and become an integral part of healthcare, regulatory agencies like the FDA will play a crucial role in shaping its impact. Ethical guidelines will also continue to evolve in response to new challenges, balancing innovation with the need for safety, fairness, and accountability. The interplay between technological advancement and regulatory oversight will define AI's future role in healthcare.

Chapter Twenty-Five

Public Perception and Adoption

Patient Attitudes, Physician Perspectives

I ntegrating Artificial Intelligence (AI) into healthcare is not merely a matter of technological innovation and regulatory compliance; it also hinges on the perceptions and attitudes of those who will be using and affected by these advancements. In this section, we delve into the complex landscape of public perception, exploring the perspectives of both patients and healthcare providers.

Patient Attitudes:

1. **Trust and Skepticism**: While many patients are excited about the prospect of faster, more accurate diagnoses and treatments, there is also a pervasive skepticism about entrusting health to "machines."

2. **Privacy Concerns**: AI often involves collecting and analyzing sensitive personal data, leading to concerns about data privacy and security.

3. **Accessibility**: There is a fear that high costs may make AI-based treatments and tools accessible only to affluent patients, widening the healthcare gap.

4. **Expectations vs. Reality**: With AI being a buzzword, some patients have inflated expectations about its capabilities, potentially leading to disappointment or mistrust.

Physician Perspectives:

1. **Efficiency Gains**: Most healthcare providers welcome the potential for AI to streamline administrative tasks and improve diagnostics, freeing up more time for patient care.

2. **Clinical Decision Support**: Physicians are generally optimistic about AI tools that can serve as a "second opinion" or offer evidence-based treatment options, especially in complex cases.

3. **Skill Displacement**: There is some apprehension about the possibility that AI could replace certain medical professions or skills, affecting job security.

4. **Ethical and Legal Liability**: Doctors are cautious about the potential ethical and legal implications of incorporating AI into their practice, including accountability for machine errors.

Conclusion:

Advantages:

1. **Informed Decision-making**: Both patients and doctors benefit from AI's ability to analyze vast amounts of data for better decision-making.

2. **Patient Engagement**: AI tools can empower patients to take more active roles in their healthcare, such as through AI-powered symptom checkers or treatment planners.

Challenges:

1. **Adoption Barriers**: Despite its potential, the adoption rate of AI in healthcare settings is slowed by patient skepticism and physicians' concerns about liability and ethics.

2. **Knowledge Gap**: The effectiveness of AI tools depends on the users' understanding of their functionalities and limitations, necessitating significant educational efforts for patients and healthcare providers.

Understanding and addressing the public's perception of AI in healthcare is essential for successfully integrating these technologies into the medical field. Strategies for education, transparent communication, and ethical consideration are vital to bridging the gap between innovation and public trust. Physicians and patients are critical stakeholders in this transformation, and their attitudes will significantly impact how AI becomes a healthcare staple.

Chapter Twenty-Six

Case Studies

Real-World Applications of AI in Healthcare

These case studies provide a practical understanding of how AI technologies revolutionize healthcare, presenting the challenges and transformative opportunities involved.

Case Study 1: Radiology and AI

Problem: Delay in diagnosis due to backlog in reading X-rays and CT scans.

Solution: An AI algorithm was developed to read radiology scans and flag anomalies, speeding up diagnosis.

Outcome: Faster diagnosis, reduced human error, and efficient utilization of radiology departments.

Case Study 2: Diabetes Management

Problem: Difficulty in managing glucose levels in diabetes patients.

Solution: A wearable AI-powered device to monitor glucose levels in real-time and alert patients.

Outcome: Better glycemic control and quality of life for diabetes patients.

Case Study 3: Mental Health Chatbots

Problem: Limited access to mental health services.

Solution: AI chatbots designed for cognitive behavioural therapy.

Outcome: Affordable and immediate mental health support for a wider population.

Case Study 4: Emergency Room Optimization

Problem: Overcrowded emergency rooms lead to delayed care.

Solution: AI-driven predictive analytics to forecast patient inflow and manage resources.

Outcome: Better patient care, reduced wait times, and efficient resource allocation.

Case Study 5: Drug Discovery

Problem: The long and costly process of new drug discovery.

Solution: AI algorithms that can simulate drug interactions and predict efficacy.

Outcome: Accelerated time-to-market for new drugs and reduced R&D costs.

Case Study 6: Remote Monitoring for Chronic Illness

Problem: Difficulty in regular monitoring of chronic conditions like heart disease.

Solution: AI-powered remote monitoring tools that continuously collect and analyze data.

Outcome: Timely interventions and reduced hospital readmissions.

Case Study 7: AI in Genome Sequencing

Problem: High cost and complexity of genome sequencing.

Solution: AI algorithms that speed up the process of genomic sequencing and data analysis.

Outcome: More accessible, personalized medicine and targeted therapies.

Case Study 8: Telemedicine and AI Diagnosis

Problem: Limited access to healthcare in remote areas.

Solution: AI-powered diagnostic tools that can be used in telemedicine consultations.

Outcome: Improved healthcare access and quality in underserved areas.

Case Study 9: Predictive Analytics for Hospital Readmissions

Problem: High rate of hospital readmissions.

Solution: AI models that predict the likelihood of readmission based on patient data.

Outcome: Targeted post-discharge interventions, reducing readmission rates.

Case Study 10: Ethical AI in Minority Health

Problem: Disparities in healthcare quality among minority populations.

Solution: AI algorithms trained on diverse datasets to minimize bias in diagnosis and treatment.

Outcome: More equitable healthcare outcomes across different demographic groups.

These case studies illustrate AI's versatile applications in healthcare, touching upon various disciplines, from radiology to mental health. Each case showcases the transformative potential of AI in addressing complex healthcare challenges while highlighting the need for ethical considerations and regulatory compliance. By examining these practical examples, we can better understand the complexities, challenges, and immense possibilities AI brings to healthcare.

Chapter
Twenty-Seven

Glossary of Terms

AI in Healthcare

Algorithm

A set of rules or procedures for solving a problem, often employed by AI systems.

Artificial Intelligence (AI)

The simulation of human intelligence processes by machines, particularly computer systems.

Big Data

Vast and complex data sets that require advanced analytics tools for interpretation and analysis.

Chatbot

A software application that can conduct a conversation with human users, often employed in mental health treatments.

Computer Vision

A field of AI that trains computers to interpret and understand visual information from the world, such as images or videos.

Data Analytics

The examination of raw data with the purpose of drawing conclusions, often using specialized systems and software.

Deep Learning

A subset of machine learning involving algorithms inspired by the structure and function of the brain called neural networks.

Electronic Health Records (EHR)

Digital records of patient health information, increasingly managed with AI tools.

Genome Sequencing

Determining the complete DNA sequence of an organism's genome, increasingly aided by AI algorithms.

Interoperability

The ability of different information systems to work together within and across organizational boundaries.

Machine Learning

A type of AI that allows systems to learn from data rather than through explicit programming.

Natural Language Processing (NLP)

A field of AI that focuses on the interaction between computers and humans through natural language.

Predictive Analytics

The use of data, algorithms, and machine learning techniques to identify the likelihood of future outcomes.

Radiology

A medical specialty that uses imaging to diagnose and treat diseases, increasingly employing AI for image interpretation.

Remote Monitoring

The collection of medical data from one location for review by a healthcare provider in another location, often facilitated by AI.

Telemedicine

Remote delivery of healthcare services, often facilitated by various forms of technology including AI.

Wearables

Devices that can be worn, like fitness trackers, that collect data on various metrics such as heart rate, activity levels, and more.

Chapter Twenty-Eight

References

Books

1. **"Deep Medicine: How Artificial Intelligence Can Make Healthcare Human Again"** by Eric Topol

   - A deep dive into the ways AI can bring empathy and humanity back into healthcare.

2. **"Artificial Intelligence in Healthcare"** by Adam Bohr and Kaveh Memarzadeh

   - Discusses the technical aspects of AI and its specific applications in medical science.

3. **"The Fourth Industrial Revolution"** by Klaus Schwab

   - A broader look at how technologies like AI are reshaping

various industries, including healthcare.

4. **"The Book of Why: The New Science of Cause and Effect"** by Judea Pearl and Dana Mackenzie

   ○ Explores the science of causality and its relevance in fields like healthcare.

5. **"Machine Learning Yearning"** by Andrew Ng

   ○ An introduction to machine learning, aimed at those who want to implement machine learning in their work.

Academic Journals

1. **Journal of Artificial Intelligence in Medicine**

   ○ Peer-reviewed articles on the latest developments in AI and healthcare.

2. **IEEE Transactions on Medical Imaging**

   ○ Focused on the role of AI in medical imaging.

3. **Nature Medicine: AI in Healthcare Special Issue**

   ○ A special issue dedicated to research and advancements in AI's application in medicine.

4. **Artificial Intelligence Review**

   ○ A broader scope that sometimes includes healthcare-related studies.

Websites and Blogs

1. MIT Technology Review: Healthcare

○ Regular updates on technological advancements in healthcare.

2. Towards Data Science

○ A Medium publication with various articles related to data science and AI in healthcare.

3. Health IT Analytics

○ News and features on healthcare technology, including AI and machine learning.

4. AI in Healthcare

○ A dedicated platform for news, features, and updates on AI in healthcare.

Online Courses

1. Coursera: AI in Healthcare Specialization

○ A comprehensive course aimed at healthcare professionals and tech enthusiasts.

2. Udacity: AI for Healthcare Nanodegree

○ A focused program on applying AI to healthcare problems.

3. edX: Principles of Machine Learning for Healthcare

- ○ Covers foundational machine learning concepts relevant to healthcare applications.

Chapter
Twenty-Nine

Summary

Embracing the New Era of AI in Healthcare

In this comprehensive guide, we have journeyed through the multifaceted landscape of Artificial Intelligence (AI) in healthcare, exploring its historical evolution, present applications, and prospects. From radiology to mental health and administrative tasks to drug discovery, the impact of AI on healthcare is profound and transformative.

We delved into the technological underpinnings, distinguishing between Artificial Intelligence, Machine Learning, and Deep Learning, and how these subsets are increasingly instrumental in healthcare innovation. Through a series of illustrative case studies, we offered real-world examples of how AI addresses complex challenges in healthcare, showcasing both the transformative potential and the ethical considerations accompanying these technologies.

Moreover, we examined the public perception and attitudes of patients and healthcare providers toward AI, underscoring the importance of trust, ethical integrity, and public engagement in this transition. We have tried to clarify the terminology associated with this field through a detailed glossary, making it more accessible to readers from diverse backgrounds.

As we stand on the threshold of this new era, you, the reader, are one step closer to fully grasping the monumental changes AI is bringing to healthcare. The advent of AI in healthcare can be likened to the discovery of fire or electricity in terms of its potential impact on human life. Just as these discoveries changed the course of human history, AI promises to redefine how we diagnose, treat, and even prevent medical conditions.

Understanding AI and its applications in healthcare is not just beneficial; it is imperative for anyone who is a stakeholder in the future of healthcare—which, in essence, is all of us. This book aims to serve as both a primer and a catalyst, encouraging informed discourse and responsible adoption of AI technologies.

Thank you for investing the time to educate yourself about this groundbreaking subject. As you close this book, know that you are better equipped to understand and engage with the transformation already underway, heralding a new paradigm in healthcare.

Welcome to the era of AI in healthcare; the future is not just promising—it is here.

www.ingramcontent.com/pod-product-compliance
Lightning Source LLC
LaVergne TN
LVHW051702050326
832903LV00032B/3956